SOLILOQUY OF AN ICE QUEEN

The Ice Queen, Volume 1

Lysz Flo

Published by Lysz Flo, 2020

While every precaution has been taken in the preparation of this book, the publisher assumes no responsibility for errors or omissions, or for damages resulting from the use of the information contained herein. SOLILOQUY OF AN ICE QUEEN First edition. March 8, 2020. Copyright © 2020 Lysz Flo.

Library of congress number: 2020903287

ISBN: 978-1734445619 Written by Lysz Flo.

Prologue 8

It Begins: Krik-Krak 9

I c e b o x   K i n g d o m 13

Welcome to the Kingdom. 15

On c e 17

Wrath 18

Envidia 19

Call Me,   BITTER 21

Dr Jekyll and Miss Hyde 24

Bitter Bitch's Brew 26

SILANS 29

He must miss me 30

The End is the Beginning 32

Re h a b 33

REVENGE 37

HE T H O U G H T   I   W O U L D

LETTING GO 41

Ailing Sobriety 43

Heart Attack: In the defense of Sobriety 49

Gladiators Weep 55

SUBLIMINALLY IN LOVE 61

Embarrassed 64

Sapiosexual Sentiments 71

Foreplay on Words 74

Please Me 78

Santeria 84

Needed Me 86

The Snowmen 93

The Illusionist 96

Ice Blocks I 100

Ice Blocks II 102

He stated he was a poet... 102

Message Undelivered 105

Forsaken Symphony 109

GOOD BYE 112

Heart for sale 115

Letter To Him, Don't Love Me 120

Heart's Inquisition 125

A Whole Damn Year 138

Hope less 145

Pitter patter 151

IF I TOLD HIM, 153

Dear love 156

3

Random Love gazing 158

DEAR SNOWMEN 162

Under this undefinable heart of glacier 173

Under these glaciers 173

is a burning Atlantis waiting to be free 173

Notes from the Author 181

Colorin Colorado Este Cuento Se Ha Acabado 174

Thank you 174

TO THE WOMAN WHO FORGOT SHE IS A GOD$_{DESS}$ 176

Epilogue 180

P o e t r y

is the only one who holds me in comfort, for pains others have no care, nor idea they caused.

P e n s

give the apologies never offered to the paper heart, crushed, for discarded consumption.

I e x h a l e in ink.

My unfallen tears and silent truths need a home – I offer you healing in my pages

It was a few days before mother's day, 2014. I couldn't be surer of *us* before then, ready to jump of the cliff, leaping in a faith that was wrong to believe. Blindly soaring on cloud nine, all by my lonesome. From then it has been a whirlwind.

A dedication, to the final event that gave me enough carbon dioxide for this queen to be made of dry ice. Dec 23, 2015 was my realization, "this is my first Christmas where Love is my own gift, to give to my-self."

A Story of the Aftermath of a Broken Heart

Those who attempt to touch me

have been left,

confused

frostbitten

D O NOT A S S U ME

Ask me how, instead

brave my storm

"To be strong never stops excluding you from humanity."

Prologue

Ignorant tongues, brand her an ice queen.

Oblivious to the expertise and dedication it takes to build such an intricate castle.

Only a queen can solely

reign through solid blocks of ice

in which she resides without faltering,

There are no seasons here

No vacation, nor holidays

Green pastures are not in bird's eye view,

All things, come to an end – Todo tiene su final

And THIS is where my birth arises,

Numbness, now takes the place of where humanity once lived, slipping slowly away like daylight in Alaskan winter,

embracing my hollowness

Night rises as I fall.

It Begins: Krik-Krak

He called me an ice queen:

    unaware of the pain in my chest

    gazing coldly in my eyes

    mirroring his allegation

    of my cold heart

    HE was guilty,

    of infusing carbon dioxide

    into my trust,

    leaving suspicious arteries

    to lack oxygen,

    f r o s t b i t e

    Even if I breathe life into him,

    he remains a frostbitten corpse,

    clothed in his delectably fed

    lies

    Gift wrapped in good faith

unaware that God has wrath

and I was to be his third-party attendant

I refurbished him,

before *me*, he was simply snow,

Now a complete man, construed with the sincerity in my fingertips,

his boyish past life; a forgotten journey into the darkness

Turned wolf, bare in his bravado of betrayal

Incriminating ME of murder in the first degree of our cultivated love

Stabbing *my* spine with an icicle, calling *me* deceitful,

while washing the blood of my naïveté down the drain

He built us an igloo, rearranging my heart in a tundra

for me to spend hope *less* nights,

Standing over my diamond encrusted oblivion,

I love you - the first of many sleet filled spells

Passion changing to subzero

The rejection in his scarce touch

become permafrost on once arduous skin

My beauty became frozen into days of yesterday's forgotten

Hail fell from my eyes

As I slept in the glacial sheets we shared

Cocooned in a child's pose

masked vulnerability

became the norm

Sincerity polluted from inside out,

HE

disgustedly afraid, for once,

his heart

was returned to his bloody hands **in ice form.**

Feeling no pain as my final words stung his ego,

'go your way : this love is lost sublimation,'

Thanks to you, I re-crown myself

The Ice Queen

"Lo que quedan son paginas con pocas letras"

-O.R.

What is left, are scarcely worded pages.

An agreement on what our love diminished too.

Icebox Kingdom

This is the paradise where

heartbroken huespedes[1]

come and so few go

Here are the remains of happiness,

the destination of clipped winged over-lovers,

hollow humans,

and daydreamers returned to reality

that love has been synonymous with misuse,

Suffering in committed crimes of self and others.

Tired organs are the entry tokens

as this will not be needed here

This.

Is my home.

Love has no place here.

Desperation calmly dropped

tattered Icarus feathers into icy rebirth

---

[1] Hotel guests

where survival is the daily goal

and woe blooms in the moonlight.

The coolness numbs that piercing pain

of passions hindrances.

Time slows and purgatory commences

within accompanied misery.

Welcome to the Kingdom.

He asks me what happened to us,

I respond,

>   I associate your failed attempt of loving me with painful PTSD.

>   The excavation of pure love from my open book of *amor*, once holding the title of freedom, is now imprisoned in anxiety, and your selfish persecution.

>   I hope this wasn't in vain, as I dressed in shame of canceled vows, removed rings, and secrets that never existed before.

>   Were my tears the best gift for your napoleon complex, when you had no other fertile land to conquer?

>   Wishing to place jagged morsels of *ayer*[2] in a pit, that holds infinite silence and contempt, my consoling prison sentences.

---

[2] yesterday

Y O U left me hollow until the echoes of your betrayal were the only memory left to complete the poisoned black hole.

You owe M E repayment for suffering, regret will come in the shoes I have bought you, dueled in Karma, preventing you to take flight,

There is no air to be caught, in the realization that emptiness will fill the hallways of y**our** house,

Y O U R entitlement will crumble to the level of your sole, soul-less, under my feet,

Who will love you when you cannot find another woman, like **me**?

We were in love

O n c e

A tragic love story

Vanished into painful memories

Wrath

I would hear her falling in love with you

with every phone call,

every text message unsent to me,

and transposed to her,

An exposed villain hiding in plain sight.

Y O U

became every lugawou[3], beneath the bed,

the dancing skeletons in my closet

of what could go wrong,

letting loose and no longer under lock and lost keys,

boogeyman

Envidia

Mi piel[4] reeks of possessiveness

Pensando que eres capaz de crear[5] summers outside of me

Causes me to cringe, my heels clicking on the icy floor at the palace,

Reminding how loud your absence is

I leave my signatures on your skin, so she can find them when you aren't looking.

Remind her that the happiness she feels with you now, is *robado*[6],

Fighting unexpectedly for first place,

Men seem to love me better

when I run against my self-dignity and sanity.

I   w   o   n   d   e   r

Does she feel like a warm breeze, to my snow storms?

Is she everything I could never be?

---

[4] My skin

[5] Thinking you are capable

[6] stolen

Does she heal the frostbitten marks

I imprint every time we create winter in different dimensions

Is *she* better than *me*?

Do you leave reminders of you behind so she, too, can smile the next day?

I would n e v e r ask this outside of monologues

Second best, seems to be all I know

Wanting to be free,

yet I always return to this captivity

circling back to you

Call Me, B　I　T　T　E　R

I do N O T want Love
Preying on me

seeing my solitude as Lonely
Wanting to keep *me* company,

Love-struck, piercing through hopeful emotions

Murdering my aspirations of becoming a we

Whispers and Professing of Idiotic Infinities
You? Love   ...Me?
It will be done and gone soon

Tattered Heart

Bruised Bits and Pieces

Nothing Manageable,

Can Be Construed...
from a Melted Snowflake

Call Me   **B**   **I**   **T**   **T**   **E**   **R**

I, a **cynic** observe words of

Devotion and *Timeless* Emotions

Emotion ₗₑₛₛ   I can only feel | **Skepticism**

Plans to Passionately Persist Have Been Relegated

My Frozen blood vessels are Emaciated

Call Me,   **A WOMAN SCORNED**

Hell! Crown *Me* an Ice Queen

for I cancel the traveled road of Empathy

Shoulders, removed...Tears Dried on Their Own

So engraved in those [He]'s leave me with every whole agape

Blood   **D r a i n e d**

Heart residing in Colder Areas

No Mental Utopia

Heading to hell-bent lunacy

Cruella: Should Be My Name

       Half Woman: Half Brutally Insane

Fighting All Godly Ways

Letting go of ^(over)-loving My Lovers
Writhing In The 7 Deadly Sins
No LONGER Lazily Lusting for Love
Envious Of Its Vain Gluttony...

Pierced by disenchanted spears of ~~love~~ gone cold
Bold Enough to Tell Me His Fabricated Truth...ending with the Ultimate...
I'll Always Love You

Call Me   **B**   **I**   **T**   **T**   **E**   **R**

For Refusing Every Ounce of Dubious Love...

Dr Jekyll and Miss Hyde

Belief, runs deep through me where hope has not taken before, if only I could construe the perfect chemical equation to make him comprehend

I am a duo-woman, bi-composed and paired emotionally, impaired

My atomic composition multiplies, nuclei and electrons in twos,

I was made for loving, carefully construed as an earth element to ground you into the reality that I can only grant surreal love, unable to explain its totality, quantum physics of what can be,

So I sit within a lab of words, elements, and positive charges, despite the negative reactions, of mis-interpretation.

I need love, to survive, a new form of symbiosis, ready and wide open to give until uncertainty closes the blinds for the light of my love to reflect through the shadows.

Confusion and disarray, I changed.

Skeptical side eye glance, to he who dances in the flickering light of the stars, the lack of confirmation cancels emotions displayed.

Disbelief leads to gates shutting to the vulnerability of my lair

The guards sharpening their weaponry

In the exterior paroles an army

Writing off lovers, beheading the trust instilled by them.

A suspect until proven innocent, condemnation when I begin to question, does he...love me or hath he forgotten thine promise of forever's, that layeth in browned rose petals, thorns replace leaves.

        Poker face infused in once rosy cheeks.

            The Ice Queen.

Bitter Bitch's Brew

When an EX-lover tells me: **he is leaving,**

You act like, I have not made disappearing acts

with souls suctioned out of their excitement to be with me

As if my heart did not know the exponents of 6
               for the feet

in which I have buried the pieces of my heart

that Lovers' tattooed TEMPORARY signatures of my permanent   <u>Eulogies</u>

Forgetting abandonment, is an easy dead end street where relationships

Can only BACK OUT OF promises

In reverse

Dressing this black widow :

As if death

does not visit the tombs of my lips

where men begged to live on
        as carcasses

I carry skeletons down my throat

like trophies,

to remember how full of emptiness

my womb is   **an overused wonderland**
where awe   **slips into frozen**
slumber

Supernatural beings like me do not blink,

exhausted eyes watching personally purchased soles

walk away unashamed

Unimpressed to believe faithful concubines will stay

Todo tiene su final, so when you announce your leave, like a best kept secret,

As if a BRUJA doesn't know her future in unclothed immortality, residuals of fidelity, left as my skin spells invocations on your tongue

Dear snowed in possibility of canceled hope,

                      I AM NOT SURPRISED AT YOUR GOODBYE'S

                            All curses have their riddance's

                             A muse is meant to be D I S C A R D E D

I remember the sounds of your laughter that stopped belonging to me while I savored Soledad's[7] company in our arctic sheets

---

[7] Loneliness personified

SILANS[8]

In the fight for our love, your push and my pull left me teeter tottering,

Confusion in the lack of recovering from the consistent pangs of tranquility that could no longer find sad single souls in this coupled equation.

Nagging was your translation of my attempts of resolution

Wallowing was my comprehension of your suffering exclusively, as if your pain was not my own,

Dejamos de ser amigos[9], allowing life to take us by the wheel making us mindless

I tried everything- this meant nothing as your uncertainty was a newly encountered trait

The words you spoke, in response to my plea, led me to this **Silans**

---

[8] SILENCE

[9] We stopped being friends

He must miss me

Making a victim out of an incomplete veteran

He attempts to find pieces of me, he didn't shred apart

There are days

we laugh at memories and he stays

staring at the shattered crystal wonderland of what will never be

He must miss

the fervor of watching the sun come alive in his hands

now a foreign fantasy

His lust an unrelated dying entity

The shoes now fitting differently in broken souls

He walk-able in abandon, as my coat of arms never carried his family name

I wonder if he can sing our songs of disappointed dominion

Feel each verse

jab his pride

that now ridicules him in empty sheets that held me

He must miss

the sincerity he could no longer reciprocate

The love he tried to negotiate with ultimatums

He must miss his misdirected crown that I placed at his feet

M   I   S   S   M   E

The End is the Beginning

You were supposed to salvar[10] me, from my broken self. Ranje'm[11], but you scattered every unfixed piece.

R e h a b

Tastes like insecurity, regret, and denial

I try to rid needing you from my skin cells

    Loneliness: an ache like fire never existed,

    Pleasure is a distant memory

Love was the only thing consistently unresponsive

    Fighting for sleep makes me sweat cold,

with un-kissed lips, unsaid words, and misguided interpretations

The demons in my mind : *what ifs and aspirations*

ringing eerily in my ear

like echoes of an abandoned ship

that never really anchors,

white flags change to prevent setting sail,

no land in the distance to plant loyalty to

Rehab is the sound of emptiness residing in the *complacency of incomplete love,*

screeching in the coldest of nights where frozen heart strings -vibrate invisibly

It's the option to not revive old bones
        closets

too packed with dying hope-less heart abuse, misuse slows its pace

Rehab isn't placed by me - it's a place by you,

where promises are broken and surprises are unpleasantly expected

        I kept telling you about the cold inside;

            you failed to realize, all I needed was a hug from you

Rehab is forgetting that you loved me, once, as much as you desired me

Remembering each time your lips denied my heart

Recalling the wonder in your eyes to be erased by its opacity

Returning to days that have gone and I now become a
        memory

Rehab reminds me that   you never chose me

As I kept injecting highs that never belonged to me, feening for any ounce dropped to me, unaware of the consequences of bewilderment, *I knew nothing felt better than us*

Until Rehab became

a silent reality that:

I lived

in rose colored glass hallucinations

Thank you for leaving me to my bettering

I never meant to enjoy painting tears

on your streak filled face of deceit.

But when my ribbons of pure love

were tainted and knotted into lies of amnesia filled forever's,

suffering filled my paintbrush and your heart,

was my delighted canvas.

R E V E N G E

I prayed for God to keep me human(e)

But for a time, hatred, was what my love was converted into,

resulted equation of your disloyalty

Nothing added up

I wanted to wipe the smug smile off your lips,

So you could taste the filling of suffering that was left in my bloated belly,

Residuals on my tongue without the desire

to indulge in nothing other than the buffet of brokenness served on a silver platter

HE THOUGHT I WOULD B E G

Succumb to him as if I didn't know he was ash

before I became the fire to finish your mother's chores,

Making you tempered glass | a solid sophisticated sculpture she would barely thank me for

Not once did he remember that I H O L D

The golden eggs

Reciprocity cracked him open into violent rays

It is amazing how mortal men cannot bathe in the same pain they cause.

I do N O T forgive your assassination of me

And still sarcastically I wish you the best,

Because no one will climb that high

Your scars whisper my name in your disturbed slumber

Your tears are white noise

that neither moves nor compels me to swallow diabetic apologies

He apologized and my icy eyes reminded him why that will be permanently insufficient,

Love is now anxiety laced in a phobia of fear of its own definition

H E S A I D, I would come back to him.

Since when, do you get offered an upgrade from Hell to leave Purgatory

Causing me to create greed with my vulnerability

On days like today,

my tears are made of flammable compositions of hydrogen.

There is no ice,

but BLUE FLAMES,

wishing to extinguish all that hurts.

I am a composition of I knew betters,

hope is a disease I rather excavate from my skin

combined with all the I shoulds

while aiming for wholesomeness

not realizing that I am more hollow rage than solidified ice.

LETTING GO

Since when

did this love

become

a　　　g　　h　　o　　s　　t　　　　o　　　f

past,

present,

and

n　　o　　　f　　u　　t　　u　　r　　e　　s　　?

I fought for us, losing in the bitter silence of distrust and deceit

the arrived end in second attempts finalizing

that winter has moved into the quinquennium of what used to be, I falter...

Ailing Sobriety

I thought I was incurable from the cold

Went to the doctor

to get prescribed a dose for this undying frostbite

Heart stopped beating

No longer pumping

Blood   c l o t t e d

Doctor said all these bottles of you would HELP

And for years I been popping extra doses of Y O U

Pain free LIVING

But the doctor never advised

that after so many years

it would become another disease.

Depending on M O R E

Momentary Gains

Stronger doses

until I stopped feeling the effects

M　o　r　p　h　I　n　e

The pain came

knocking the wind out of me,

Catching me by surprise,

Resulting in weight gain, deep depression, chest pains, and shortness of breath.

I never knew that this insomnia would attack me so deep

The co-dependency
       I have lost myself

in this thing I have with you...Since it feels single sided.

Why didn't you take away the pain?

Crying senselessly,

Feening for the quick **fix.**

Killing the pain, temporarily.

Your bottles become E M P T Y

Running out of refills.

Forgetting my well-being is N O T in

Y
O
U

Going from place to place with your prescription.

Yet you are D O N E.

When I am j u s t getting started

Walking around like the dearly departed.

Getting the shakes as I rub my hands across your label.

Unstable, I stare into the empty medicine cabinet

 Not O N E pill left.

Cold sweats and INSOMNIA

Why did you come in like you would save me?

 Keep me healthy when all you did was worsen my sickness.

Ignoring the fine print

Organs failing, immunity disintegrating

      Who will cure ME of the Side Effects of YOU?

I wanted to fill your starvation but I was
too transparent
to[o] empty
myself into you.
Too hollowed within, to be a source
instead I was a lacking option.

Watching you be hungry,
because what I offer isn't palatable enough to [y]our brokenness.
I apologize for not showing you how to hunt instead.

You have become the warmth of my sheets and the shape of my pillows
My peace in daydreams trapped in the now nightmare
of mornings where I wait for you to ring the doorbell
-an evaporated reality-

I remember why I stopped listening to love songs
 I never needed a reminder of how much I love you
In order to move on,
I trapped it away.
Until, I could no longer find my way back to feeling the same

Heart Attack: In the defense of Sobriety[12]

I have been told by a dear friend| there is strength in accepting vulnerability

I accept.   'I never been here before.'

I never imagined love

would have brought me to my knees in the darkness,

Beyond consolation as if I were living in death,

I could not reach the phone to call an ambulance.

Yet you froze

As I was mourning and even to this moment, you never noticed, my suffering

Surprised that I feel, like,

everything we built has been sent to a shredder

to then be incinerated

so the only thing LEFT is **smoke and dust.**

Unable to cough,

Unable to breath,

---

[12] Title "Heart Attack" by Trey Songz

The oxygen you offered before disintegrated into Carbon Dioxide.

Remembrances of us,

I fear, incapability of being happy beside you as I once was,

My ticker now a ticking time bomb

You admitting my improper introduction

of the shocking pain that numbs my arms

Preventing from letting you go

simultaneously letting you stay.

While wanting to leave

You, Clogging my arteries

as you felt suffocated

I, wishing to do CPR,

You preferred the emergency room.

Left me waiting outside, In the cold, Without you.

I never knew that the sharpest pain is from regretting the day I said "I love you" back.

Fighting against the world as they could not see the diamond in you,

I never knew love would

H U R T this bad.

I cannot believe we made it this far,

Planning the next steps of our lives, Hand in hand,

Then you decided to let go, all on your own.

Did you forget your promise to keep me happy?

Watching in horror,

As my eyes lose the glint, my signs of life weak,

Reaching out to you, hoping you would think it through.

Feeling the sharp explosion in my chest as it all crumbles,

How can I be sure you won't cut off my life support when all I lived for, was you.

Accepting the signs of short term memory, forgetting about me. Going in and out of consciousness. Yet the platelets we believed to flow through freely, were building up.

Slowly letting go of the blows to each other| Fighting without resolution.

Accepting. **Defeat.**

Why must I keep trying to reactivate your heart while mine kept losing its beat?

My lips now blue...because you decided without me. B E T R A Y E D you say. What about me?

Leaving me on the rescue truck   For someone else to save me.

You were supposed to heal me. Nurse me back to recovery.

My heart shivers in the confines of its new home. I would give it all to be discharged and go back home. But you leave my respiration up to the machines.

Why do you visit me in hospice? When you caused this? Having the ability to transplant the missing piece of my heart, that you nonchalantly kept.

Holding back the tears as you see me on my deathbed

Yet afraid to return the warmth, I need, preventing my blood flow.

Worst pain that I ever had

                              Afraid to let go

Too Scared to keep going. I accept the vulnerability.

But never knew the love you gave me would feel like a heart attack.

Capable of Killing, with the possibility of Recovery

When lovers say you don't know them -

Tell them - I know your silence
The burdens you carry
that crush you on the hills
you walk barefoot on

I've walked beside your shoes
without you glancing at me

I have been the cross roads and the path unchosen

I have seen you disappear and appear from uncertainty

Your frequency shifts me undesirably

If I paid enough attention
to the echoes of suppressed soliloquies
I could hear the thoughts in each heartbeat

I dream of you in truths hidden consciously

I may not know the dances you have made with your demons
but each time we meet eyes
I see them hold you back from me

Gladiators Weep

In a field of skulls, flooded by beautiful deaths and glory.

The sound is never heard and the sight, never seen.

Colossus shrinks to an actual human being.

The trees bare of leaves and the wind is still, no sound of rustling.

A gladiator, in all premium armor stoops.

Medals and proof of wars won, yet no one notices, that in the behemoth like valor.

There is a war that is constantly lost.

Who could possibly comprehend that aggression is a defense mechanism

Or that the coldness, dispersed upon bloody blades and shattered skulls hide the mush inside.

I have been ripped from my home

not one comprehends that with the arrogance in my smile,

my gut wrenching truth gets shielded inside.

The crowd becomes fog and the sun forgotten.

Compelled and swallowed by the darkness that caves in around dawn and

amplifies after midnight.

The wounds heal yet the injuries remain skin deep. Every time I get saved, a piece is missing from me.

The faces change-soldiers lost-only to be replaced

War is the same.

Tarnish-meant maintains the same resemblance

The sound echoes among-st wolves howls and crickets chirping

Drowned by nature

Solitude holds me in discomfort

    I   a   Gladiator   Weeps

As tears dry in the cold of the night

feasting on the scabs within the wells of my Frankenstein like pacemaker.

I become an emptiness I am unable to share.

I have had my soul pillaged by wolves in Sheep's and emperor's clothes. Conniving paupers made to believe themselves, Kings

not once reciprocated for my loyalty.

AS   -IT-

WAS ALWAYS EXPECTED OF ME.

I

Weep

A woman, hidden under armor that holds only the finest metals and stones

Resilience during the day

Stumbling on the world's weight in the evening

ASHAMED

This Gladiator WEEPS

In the gallows with death surrounding me for comfort

The burden of strength is easier to carry than my own extinction in shadowing vulnerability, not once, asked if I am hurting.

I   LOSE   EACH   TIME.

The admirers evaporate and the success is a whisper to a shattering ego.

As

This

Gladiator

Weeps

Quietly

With dry eyes

Dear death, you have become

  the bouquet of flowers

                                        I gift

        to new lovers and friends:

as expectations seeded in what this growth will be

I fell in love with a poet once and he rewrote me into unfinished poems that always had possibilities

Never retouching the lines yet always finishing with an ellipses as the end so hope was it's best ink drawings on my heart

I loved him like syllables, breaking his every detail down until his next evolution was a new path to follow him too - unable to settle into any other genius mind much to my chagrin, he was unique and memorable

...and intangible

I can wish to unlove you in any language I know and still I have no definition for this curse - so I await next lifetimes to see if I'll be first...

how could you meet my eyes and not shudder simultaneously, how could these love poems not trail back to you, to find me.

SUBLIMINALLY IN LOVE

When two poets love
          we never speak,
         we write
             declarations of love that we will never hear

     We promise eternity in silence

    Passion is undying like our ink
We keep expense-ing our futures into aching nothingness

          Fear
holds our hand instead of us doing so in real time

We subconsciously need without consciously accepting it

Loving as two poets is a roller coaster of unexpressed emotions

           A death so beautiful we keep repeating it
                    instead of letting go

      Never interlocking fingers,
afraid of our written truths being transmitted through touch

Worried about the nudity of our souls,
  only allowing our skin to be the vulnerability, we only know

        tell him
he forms the curvature of my words when describing love
        in my handwritten prose

Someone recite what I never could, so he could see the infinity drawn in these subliminal sentences etched into his understanding

Memories
Meant to be read
by unknowing eyes just to know how beautiful you look in mine

Someone
turn on the microphone to my beating heart
while I hide my guilt, despite each thump
 spelling out his name every time

Our actions too loud and simultaneous
Our acceptance too blinded by past lives
Our hope too naive for our age
Our ability too constricted for self placed prisoners

As two poets, we write forever to never make it right into today
When Love is the synonym, we are too shaken, for us to speak aloud into existence.

And I love him, even when our silence is too sharp for my pastry heart

When the world says he isn't worthy and my dulled pride
fights the urges of him
My heart beats at the sight of his photo

Embarrassed

I am embarrassed at how in love I am with you
so my eyes hide from your visibility to deter my truth

That my heart is your upper hand

placed in China glasses at your fingertips to be coiled at your disposal

I fall victim to your past pains	inflicted
Canceling notions of us with	never
Erasing the inept outside of	love
Leaving me to enjoy my the amor	voyeurism in

I have to give you

Watching too deeply into signals and being told

I was always driving the wrong way

your heart

Has always been

 the wrong turn

I wanted, my dead ends, to be born in

Ashamed of diving head first into an oasis

Because I had been dehydrated
from self-admiration

My chest has become a jukebox of love
songs

that carry names of forgotten
laughter and faded feelings

hoping for a coin of hope to play freely

Hope is a one way street that only leads to u-turns to
nowhere

I fell in love with a fallen hero

I am my mother's daughter a lover of casos perdidos,

who enjoy breaking into my heart instead of
cradling my offering

I am my grandmother's child enjoying the
darkness of loss

reminiscing on days that will never return

and telling stories of how disappointment
is to be expected

                                        giving to never receive

I am my Godmothers reflection,

grief bathed in waiting smiles and tired eyes,

mourning is our best dress and tragedy the only shoes

we get to wear as sacrifice is the price to feel it has all changed

I am my father's daughter who would wait until the next past life

for true love to always return and be new again,

tearily awaiting departure stubbornly ignoring my decomposition.

      I am just fine

Salacious Idiosyncrasies

Heal this fire between the path of lust and no return, etched on the goosebumps of my skin

Before the Ice, I was a rampant fire of passionate addiction for each one of them.

I want to pay my thoughts in skin instead of pennies,

To take each pensive inch onto taste buds

absorbing the leaks of brainstorms with lubricious lips

Can I?   Lick the sense out of your brain cells

Digest the stream of sapiosexual banter that makes my mouth water

And thirst, constrict my throat as I attempt to swallow these pensive moments whole

I fetishize him into pools of desire no one else swims in
Craving him like Lust, knows he is my favorite drug addiction
Wishing him to sleep in it
Formulate his whole existence into the depth of my surrender
Savoring his skin, like I have been in a desert
Dehydrated in angst
I need it
To satiate the sex that leaves me at peace
Calming the fire within me for the time being
Replaying the recordings of my memories
I can't help the enjoyment of hearing the moans I make for him
The exasperation of pleasure from him
The physical tremors
Two fiends severely salacious

I, too, want more.

Have you ever?
Closed your eyes, bit your lip, and meditated into an out of body experience-
While remembering the delectable indulgence of passion

I woke up like this,

A bubbling cauldron of sexual energy

Filled to the brim and boiling hot spells of desire to spill onto kissable lips

Baritone banter, a solid phallic instrument of pleasure

                              Sheets twisted around me like a prison

                                    where nakedness

                            does not reach out far enough to become

                                       a separate individual

Wanton wants where we were last

Wicked laughs and

Sexy smirks

Wishing for whimpers

                                              Lust-full leakage

                                              Fist-full of sheets

                                                 Mercy denied

Throat dressed in large fingers

Salaciously rising out of slumber

                                        I woke up like this –

Sapiosexual Sentiments

Can I release my inner sapiosexual?

I've been watching how your frontal lobe carries on

creating forbidden thoughts into flexible fruition.

Fruit

for its picking

as your mind is shared on pages for all to see and

few

to comprehend

T   h   i   r   s   t   y

for the knowledge that drips

from your medulla oblongata

You please me,

with every fellatio filled phrase that bares neurons

Naked is your nucleus under creativity, I'd **l o v e** to savor the intensity of your brain cells

I hope you don't take it wrong

When I want to raise your brain

to new heights in a storm you have *never* encountered before

Flooding with liquefied ideas

Let me come

Construe concepts under copious constriction

As I visualize

what your education tastes like,

translating into salacious sound

Pen strokes leak knowledge that is hard to swallow

Your diction-ary is thick with explicit vocabulary

I wish to study closely

I want to learn the Braille version of your thesaurus

redefining what I am feeling

through your responsive exclamation of appreciation

rolling my tongue in Rated R phrases

A rebellious pupil requesting punishment,

Detain and Dictate me to go from italic to bold

<u>Underline</u> my curves

manipulated in large hands

becoming cursive font to fondle brainwaves

A sucker to your intellect

I wonder have I absorbed it all yet- while lips let chocolate ink drips

seep of humid ideas and penetrating concepts

I stop you mid-sentence to ask you if you'd like to know what it feels like to sleep within mental moistness, leaking knowledge of biology

As the study becomes anatomy,

allow me to release my inner sapiosexual

Foreplay on Words

I hope that you don't take this wrong

But...I been...thinking... Of finding how many ways...

I can intertwine with the pronunciation of your Syllables

Cunning linguistic conversations between (lips)

Feeling your words arrange seductively

Intellectually stimulated into salacious verbiage

-Dominant demands-

Allow me to bring to life my soliloquy

performed in solitude

Awaiting recognition for the submission
|To my favored pen|

Willing the ink to refill and reuse

Literal context clues permeate the plethora of phallic fantasies

I can't help but brainstorm upon
Repetitious Midnight Reflections

Defining the ellipses with adverbs.

A Continuum of climactic words

To coerce... Disorientation,

Reverting to the top of the page

Reiterating all the phrases

Practicing until perfection.

To flow **your** tip on fresh pages.

Be my subject and I, Your predicate

For(e) the play on words.

My body screams your name before my vocal chords emote the sounds of agreement into duo occupied sheets

Recalling how you please me

There are cravings food cannot fulfill

*Do my moans ever wake you
in the middle of the night,
Among my carnal cravings seeping
from my pores,
Does your body
recall that you are missing
from your home
where my warmth is,
reaching out to me subconsciously,*

*Your taste buds
must salivate like mine,
at the recollection of
my skin melting against your ravenous tongue,*

*Do sly smiles form,
at evil grins and intoxicating exclamations,
dancing sensually in the shadows of your memories,*

*Aren't you
Unable to forget,
you belong to me.*

Please Me

Instructed to advise how much I'd like to

please myself with you

allow me to explain

the depth of my desires

that are in your sole proprietorship

Pleasure is actually all mine

-in my point of view of your satisfaction-

I succumb to serve you

Allow me to

relish in our secret desires

Fulfilled betwixt submission and dominance.

Please don't misunderstand

the need to savor you with or without command.

I simply attempt, to reconnect our minds

synchronizing mutual satiation every time.

Return you back to past lives

reminding you why

we are currently in the present.

I want to become the missing piece

to the void of your cravings

Saturate me

with every drop of the world's weight on your shoulders and

take in the endorphin's that alleviate your stress.

Y O U

make knees unresponsive and legs shake

because the earth displaces

as you reach undiscovered galaxies with every thrust

of your shuttle.

Defy gravity with me in unison

As only I have been proclaimed to cater to your untapped desires.

I await you

To   -put your tongue on my body-

There is nothing better than

my fantasies coming alive in fire burning flesh

As groans escape flawlessly heart wrenching lips.

May I

converse with your pent-up frustration

to the point of release

My need to possess you is passively aggressive.

Fascinating your eyes with bit down lips and unseen reactions.

This freaking, is only a peep show for you.

Locked in my room awakening to the mutual jonesing

my favorite flavor drips down my taste buds

as the feeling of you has been braised on my body.

Successfully ensuring that I only require you

to replenish my sensual overflow with the delectable-ness of your body.

You Fit Me So Perfectly

Love ignites at silent glances

blazes with touch our body language can't help to scream in slow motion

Allow my passion to blur with emotions that I am unable to display in un-coerced actions

Give me permission to be drowned out by musical melodies.

Exclamations of ownership accepted

escape full lips

I've been living through hot spring

rain since our last physical conversation

Patiently waiting for you to begin your sentence of summoning me

Until then Sir, I can imagine you bringing what's rightfully mine to me

so I can please myself with your body.

I want to make love with you until
Your solace no longer quantifies your freedom
Cultivate love until your newly discovered wings stretch out in its magnificence the air beneath foreign yet captivating defines what self-love is - including us to be equated to loving yourself
Sorrow has lulled me to sleep on occasions where your sunlight has inked away

Santeria

He called it Santeria,

The way I had incantations of love,

Spilling in the sacrifices I made nightly,

Around embers where our bodies lit up rooms that had no windows,

He worships me in his subconscious,

Consciously feasting on bended knee

A ritual familiar to the dawn not once setting desires in liberation,

The capability to see his destiny draped in greatness

tainting my reality of letting go,

He and I partaking in libations

to remain addicts of half love

Vodoun Romance,

unable to release, fearing the worst, delving deeper,

I have died many times and was returned from this fate,

For him.

There are lipstick stains I have yet to leave on your skin

Promises of pleasure unmade

Stay a little longer

Needed Me

He called me BRUJA, my eyes become his incantations

my contorted lips are spells of oblivion

In which he continuously chose

to be a faithful concubine to,

Unaware that my pot of elixirs mix at molten temperatures

my chants of unspoken love and echoing passions

would burn us alive

Increasing dosages

Mutually running out of intact sheets

to hold him in the clutch of a Voodoo Priestess.

This love supplies

combustion of broken hearts and regret.

No alchemy could rehash forever's that remain unmet.

You Belong To Me,

In The height of the night - when my fingers move you like puppetry

moans are spells that keep your vision blurry,

The haze of lust slipping from skin to skin interaction,

It is an addiction

And then I ask my self do I love them cold and unavailable because I am accustomed to the ice in my chest ? Keeping it safe from condensation?

Intro to Snowmen

He battles daily against the servitude
he was awarded
Fighting for royalty
to be broken
at home,
a place
where time is cooked, cut, and distributed.

Loss is now systematic with revenge coping,
a lone soldier in untrustworthy streets,
sadness does not live in the deep darkness, it comforts him
Has him, fighting against Lucifer's piece of the Pie.
Warring for the Golden Green Ticket
to end the vicious cycle of extinction
PEACE
A set-up, for failure,
few pass the exams of code of conduct,
all you can get are perfect attendance certificates tattooed
on the exposed parts of his soul.

Amor de la Bajura

No strangers allowed

Do you think you are another deli number

Continuum of who has visited my most precious offerings for your fill to be met

Acting as overtly salacious spare

faking no strings attached

knowingly delving into shallow passion

Emotional depths

naming us puppets of love

that neither will accept nor dispel it into existence

They'd say the lust on my fingers resemble dry ice burns, loveless motions in the dark

Using their affliction for survival and sucking souls to keep warm for tomorrow

My emotions discarded on the shaving of my concealed ticker

Not once noticing

my words are deflectors of pain

my actions are lie detectors

radically reshaping the truth

that love is hardest to display when tears

have been frozen to your face and disbelief is all that I can come by

I have been fooled for so long that feeling loved by someone

is an exhilarating confusion stagnating me into silence

I have exploded inside

attempting to blow down the blocks cemented around my heart

I've attempted to reach for you, panicking through anxiety filled residue of abuse

but didn't have the heart to ask to be rescued

So outside you see an Ice Queen

jabbing your heart strings with ice picks of uncaring phrases,

Love eats away at my soul to the point

I have no return, either defrost or live within a tundra of solitude

My feelings are so robust

that vulnerability is a war

I rather fight against

than be openly free to

repetitive assassinations of disappointment

Able am I, to run,

for cover and take the pain of frost bitten skin

sucking love away, ridding me of oxygen

Suffering in silence is home

The men in my life have a habit of disappointing women,

for they need to dehumanize their creator to forget they <u>aren't gods.</u>

To feel more potent than their bone chilling insecurities

The Snowmen

I have mourned many decayed infatuations, yet ours is the one

I consistently grieve^{x2}

our un-conceived love for centuries.

And he knew, unable to meet my eyes and unwilling to show

mine, I ,a, super heroine,

addicted to kryptonite that came distilled from the place of

love, he never took me to see,

Or the uncomfortable silence in unkissed lips, a fool for his

embrace, and a marionette under his enchantment, I

wanted to love him like a displaced person finding home,

Like the caretaker of lilies during the harshest winter, I

wanted to get to see you spring into the beauty hidden

under the ice,

Placed aside

like a broken tarnished sunflower without glow, they wonder where the thorns came from as the budding rose cemented into the deepest crevice of the earth,

A ray of sun shine to never be found, finding comfort in the valley of shadows.

What do you do when are addicted to Kryptonite?

The Illusionist
Recalling his first show

Consuming every fiber of my being
Engulfing electrons within my neutrons,

Converting reality into an animated propensity...
Where 4D was convincing

No longer questioning abstract emotions

Fortifying preconceived notions, fulfilling the 5 questions
Determination enveloped within misconstrued abominations

He included me, subconsciously within his most aspiring act
An Act

Of Flawless Animated Execution
Where Carnal Fervor and Sentimental Vehemence
Become Material for the Point

Souls are Solidified within an Invisible Crystal
how divine!

I Thought to Be Internally Secure

Turmoil did Seemingly Cease

Regarding this Ultimate Master   piece.

In A Transfixed Mental State

Believing of such realistic mounds of devotions

seeded within My Thalamus.

Miraculous Re-Wiring and Re-gluing of Glial Cells...

To Fit His Accordance...Of Self Proclaimed Importance

I live with the Executioner and He simply in love with What Seems Like Me...
Execution superiorly chosen

He Fastidiously...Researched and Rehearsed...at such Extremities.

Sacrificing Potentialities to...Intellectual Advancing...
Ignoring His Susceptibility

The Illusionist Lost in the Voids of Reality...
Filled in Cognitive Technicalities.

Without Remorse Nor Judgmental Calamity
Did He Release ME from

Mis-Impression

Mis-Representation
Mis-Communication
Mis-Interpretation
Mis-Direction

Piercing Me...From Behind Yet Right In Front of My Spines most Distanced Organ

Ribs Could Not Protect It...

I Remained in Ignis Fatuus.
Partially Meditative Status...Without Seeing Clearly...

Until What Seemed Summoned by Past Passion now Prostrated Poltergeists...
Laid Upon Me....His Heel Of Achilles

His Illusions and Fabrications of Palpable Fantasies Chanting Reclusively...Upon His Own World

Loneliness Needs No Altercation...Despite My Discomposure To His Fallacies

Foolishly....I Remain Naught
Lest He...Search Endlessly....For Another Act of Benign Executions...Leading to Individualistic Perfections

An Illusionist Remains A Vampire...Insatiable with No Reflection...

I Watch

From the Sidelines...Awe-struck by his Execution...

Quietly recalling His First Show...

Rabbits No Longer...Appear from Thin Air
Spirits are too disconnected to such Calumniation

No longer enveloped in fruition...

His Own Illusions, His Termination

Ice Blocks I

Few have lived to bury their bones inside my womb for comfort

Fornication of emptied emotional wells

bloom into forgotten responsibilities

I have birthed them new lives of addiction

Kryptonite cocktails to be savored in secret

as their fantasies are filled to the brim

their memories carry only my name

My skin has the DNA of a voodoo priest dipped in milk-less chocolate

Ink drops of poetic justice

leave enchantments in their sheets, still dripping from their chin

Even if tomorrow's promise of abandonment signed deeply into my Scars came, I'd smile still at the beautiful webs of mosaic love attempts we made on our way to this dead end

I rejoice in the oxygenated rainbow of hope I see in your shyness, living for your laughter and dying for your desire. Burn into me beautiful time stamps of what my dreams never fathomed.

This intimacy, a platinum constellation to remain in my heart safely for a lifetime, no matter how the pulse makes the clock tick.

I love you, before it becomes multilingual exclamations in pheromone filled sheets and lifetime recollections

Ice Blocks II

To be loved by a poet is to suffer painful reincarnations of unforgotten scars, continuously self-inflicted in immortal phonetics, to be a muse is to be the trophy of emotional deaths and births of momentary, happy, insanity.

Nonetheless love is excruciatingly consuming and a necessity, therefore, consider yourself a mythological creature...until the fable is finished

I was left with dried ink for I love you's that had no synonyms, looking for a continuation of adverbs without noticing that the season changed from spring to a sunless winter.

The final sunset cast away stones into a humble soul, transformed into a tyrant

He stated he was a poet...

I believed him when he manipulated syllables with his tongue

life itself came from the existence in historical cunning context

Shakespearean soliloquies dripped from his lips

Not once a pause or missed hymn as he resuscitated in the contours of my tropical oasis

Hands leading me to believe that hieroglyphics were once drawn by him

                I transformed Into his art

Becoming immortal in reaction to his connotations

      He must be a proliferation of writers combined in one being

I became his pen and paper,   as he chases storms,
      his brain continuing to fulfill himself with food for thought

This patience to paint notes on skin with the simple flick of a wrist

Taking me to new flights of intellectual stimulation

Self-introspection took a vacation

displacing me into a frenzy of rhythmic rituals

in the visuals of his conversation

                        He has to be an artist

placing me into a gallery

Outlining loins for his viewing pleasure

Renaissance man

that restrains me from |escaping|

the utter brilliance of being re-sculpted into

the arches and twists he prefers in the delivery of linguistics

He preferred execution over description

until the words have run out and all

he's left me with is a trickling ellipses

The beginning of literature to be taught when loving a poet.

Message Undelivered

I dreamed of love

made from soap operas and poetry

                Busy in love

with beautiful dudes in distress, trying to save the more broken of them

                Falling for

short term happily ever afters and broken promises

                              I saw love in his eyes once,

                                  that was unrecognizable

noticing the glint, fades from time to time

                How could I,

recognize the love in his eyes

if all I've known were of its false prototypes?

All I have ever seen were the prostheses,

compared to feeling ablaze within

with just one shy look and goofy smile,

lost in his fixated gaze

 My glow reflected the fire you silently had inside.

I used to see myself.

in the windows of your soul

after regretful decisions, I remain an alien form to see truth displayed in affliction

                        I chose in error to remain oblivious.

he now has dreamy empty eyes

lacking sleep, in the cravings of yesterday

I stare at pictures

noticing the smoke where light once flickered

I regret not once loving you, nor meeting you,

but becoming a rough draft of your personification of love

crossing out and rewriting should haves and could haves,

Unable to add final chapters

to happily ever afters written and published

in my head.

Mutually unable to rehash lost pages, left unread,

so I attempt to revive emotional unavailability, somehow

I can't stop dreaming of what could have been

since what will *be,* slowly disperses in a comfort of silence,

Over giving to credit back the moments I took so much away,

Disney seems to be the closest I get to wishing upon stars
for un-created constellations

I wanted to etch you

into the bind of the book of our past lives

to ensure you'd remain the back bone of our own mythological futures

Desiring to remain

as the watermarks to stay imprinted and

leave memories as deep as my ocean pools of love for you.

Yet here I remain with eraser in hand and blotted sheets comprehending that

Forevers' are temporary fashion tattoos that fade as the pain lasts longer

by receiving refunds to expenses I never felt as sacrifices.

Consistently feeling foolish and taking blows- as if I never meant anything to you-

How could you, if your thesaurus of love had teardrops to blur it's definition ?

Walking away slowly,

I log out of this unspoken soliloquy

my words carry no weight despite how heavy they seem

when they leave my chest and return overlooked

   Tucking in pages of spoken secrets. Message undelivered.

Forsaken Symphony

I have given up playing symphonies

Retire my skin

as the ultimate instrument

in which I continue relying on orchestras for comfort

cutting the s t r i n g s

to no longer bleed from replacing sad playing violins

I swim in pools of tears that n e v e r fall

Bathe in saline

that dehydrates the suppleness of my skin

To no longer be appetizing

to false hopes and limited time forever's

I disconnect the speakers

where my heartbeat echoed through his chest

and copious cacophonous memories are the tunes

emitting from my burdened shoulders

I think of the conductors

who knew how effortlessly to lead me into

holograms of perfection

I remember maestros

who made harps out of sweeping me off my feet until

Gravity was no longer an issue

I remember the distant stares of players

who knew how to sway me to and fro through artistic manipulation

The sweetest notes of woe to escape lips

as the pain sounded so beautiful,

the numbness made it all bearable to be their concerto,

an object of classical infliction

The golden instrument now gathers dust-

in unplayable reveries

Just replaying the scars of every

carving away and chipping

I hand in the bloody sheet music of my sincere soul into subzero fire,

a PHOENIX, adversely born - into an ice queen

no longer a symphony to be played

G O O D   B Y E

seems to be the favorite word to never say

Covering winter time with the summer memories

Putting disjointed hands to constellations built apart.

Good, as if riddance is as easy as driving by what used to be and never will

Bye, to the Dream turned into hallucination

lies to a hopeful heart, too blind for reality

So void fills the empty space left in yester- days and i

walk towards the rainbow apart from cloudy skies and light rain.

Fare isn't the way of life but be well.

I didn't want a poem to stay stuck in your frozen memory of finished catharsis

I wanted spoken word,

I wanted to be performed, revised, revisited, and memorized by heart.

Sometimes I feel like I can feel your thoughts

discounting them into hallucinogens of hope

That doesn't belong here.

He taught me how to feel Love in English.

Giving it a meaning, but like all foreign things, did it ever. Belong to me?

Wasn't it inconsistent with the accents I preferred to express full devotion.

Stolen heart

excavated for its remnants.

Foreigner

staking claim against all that isn't in your roots.

Conqueror of feelings you never needed responsibility for, a thief.

Loving a prototype is a test run on how deep you can drown before you flow with the correct current and float.

Everyone mentions how love made them non-believers.

My numbness isn't a fear of loving nor being loved.

But of the stoic look of emptiness, feared

Amid-st the illusionists, who profess the use of a word.

that has become decrepit in flesh ridden lips.

Becoming a death to the abundance of hope

that once lived in a warm body,

carrying smiles like her permanent signature now banished to bygones.

Heart for sale

I have a refurbished heart for sale,

Anyone want to a buy a Corazón?

It's not shiny nor new

Much wear and tear from the strenuous activity of

incorrect inclination

I got a heart for sale,

See it pumps rather loudly so even in silence...it could be heard

Yet no one listened,

It pushes forth even when it's faint

Fuming for love like a locomotive,

and the dents?

...well...they are deep

because that's how hard it goes without choice, who else will

I have a heart para venta-

And today---IT no longer suits me

Voluntarily, I GAVE...and silence STOLE its composition, return to sender, left me sewing over opened wounds, the stitched scars show it's consistent resilience given that I've provided all pieces left to who was holding it hostage,

I got a heart for sale,

There's nothing wrong with it. But rid me of it. Before it meets a beautiful death worth the ashes beyond the aorta,

I find my lungs, filled with toxic disappointment seem to be tarnishing veins

So I sell it, before it cannot be transplanted to someone who can stand the use of it. A hopeless romantic able to give what I no longer have

as I, have reached the maximum potential of its use.

No more miles to add!

No MORE road left to TRAVEL

I got a heart for sale,

Treat this heart gently, as it has the victories of war yet it bruises rather easily.

m'ap vann yon kè[13],

You ask me why I trade it, for the root of all evil, yet evil has been rooting since I implanted my heart into someone's hand to hold gently and they have dropped it intentionally- or naught either way, I have a heart for sale

The money I receive is ENOUGH for me To USE without feeling guilt, fear, regret or resentment.

How can I keep this heart if I cannot feel it beating nor hear it. I don't feel its vitality.

---

[13] I'm selling a heart

Yet outside of me it plays symphonies of leftover hymns waiting for reciprocation that I-

cannot offer to it.

An instrument in which I cannot fine tune to the silence I feel inside

I rather not let it die, so I try in the black market of lovers who still have hope,

I had a heart that needs love like a fiend needs dope to continue, but I stopped injecting what consumed me,

in exchange I embrace this hollow space within,

I have a heart for sale!

Dame tu mejor oferta, Give ME your BEST offer, Because your purchase will ALWAYS be more than the negatives balances that were awarded to me.

I cut my losses, cashing out on my brokenness, leave me empty, without this useless organ.

In the end

I-

I still win

emotionally bankrupt

I ask again,

does anybody want to buy a heart?

Letter To Him, Don't Love Me

No me ames,

If my words do not carry the weight of gold, that my pure heart tends to melt at the seams, erupting lava filled dissertations, within my beating heart strings that never reach fruition.

Reading without comprehension, that every diamond encrusted word, has been pressured into confinement excavating

within to let them out, love me not, if they cannot reflect the light I had inside in your eyes,

Do not love me, if you cannot see my fears hidden behind, the weakened moments where I act my strongest, to prevent myself from crumbling into the coal, where soot of life's hardships prevent me from feeling my best,

 Don't love me if you are too weak to lift me from the lost maze of self conscious disappointments, that have created welts in my courage,

I will fight until your doubt crowds my reality,

u n r e e l   m e   a s   I   r e e l   a w a y .

I sometimes trip on my way to go towards you, thorned with perceptions and what ifs embedded into the imprints of my fingertips, all I have is not what you expected.

You aren't the only one with chunks missing as you carry on wounded, i have the will to endure more pain as the rearranging of pieces can be brutal. But i know no other way to take flight than to keep flying into combustion of re-composition,

P a   R e n m e n   M w e n

if you cannot comprehend the language of my relentless pushing to the finish line of the beginning to forever.

If forever can be a math problem you **can** find a solution to, walk away Because X + Y is not why I need to see you beside me.

Love me not, if my silent pleas of disbelief are too heavy to bear, and the loudness of my internal struggles aren't music to your ears,

Tell me if you are not strong enough to carry too much weight, I am heavy.

Because love is what I do not take lightly.

Leave me - if you cannot keep choosing me, despite the lack of laughter on harder days and rough patches.

I have been known to raise my men from the death of hopelessness and make them Kings of society.

I am no meager woman. No me ames, if abundance of fulfillment is too hard to sift through my complications for.

N o m e a m e s

if you have cases of chronic abandonment, I have no room nor space for murderers of an over loving soul, that gives selflessly even if I cannot prance in an abundance of emotions, that forgive you when there aren't ashes of innocence.

Some call me a fool, yet I say, the one who decides to love me **proactively** will see that there lies a sapphire within the titanium fortress I have built.

Do not offer me empty words decorated by affliction, love is:

Everything needed to make humanity better,

Death to Egos, and a hot soup of Pride swallowed

Compromise and not sacrifice,

Eternal even if you leave my side, it never ends inside,

Getting a biggest supporter when you cannot even fathom the greatness inside you,

Accountability and consistency,

To me love is, what i have been created for, therefore, if this is intelligible, please, save your introduction and walk away from me, and don't you dare take part, in loving me emptily.

Better yet, don't love me.

No one counts the amount of snowflakes that fall from the sky, but looks in disgust at the snow dirtied by the earth,

Forgetting that [they] carried wonder before they fell,

Then I understood that my scraps were not the whole morsels I believed to be offering but leftovers of self
I scramble to assemble, to paint a pretty picture.
Games lost and goals of instant gratification played, wondering how do I stop playing this sonance of somber suffering unrealized?
How do I find, my way, back to loving you...dear us, dear self.

Fight for Sobriety

Heart's Inquisition

What do you do when you have an immense heart

Unable to display the crate of love songs it can't sing to anyone?

Unfit to dance accompanied in the rain, carrying so much light in its place that has to be put away

Swallowing the gulps of suppressed I love yous

Que hago?

Having to clip the immensity of its wings because there's nowhere to go- grounded and waiting for liftoff

To love loudly is its only design ill-fitted to be placed upon on a billboard in all its splendor

Ki sa'm pou Mwen fe?

I fear not the magnitude of love but that it may crush the respondent

Too intense to float in the sea of happiness given, leading him ashore to leave me again

Lost in my own depth

Sink in Peace

I don't apologize for your inability to swim and lack of equipment,

I'm not hard to love, my heart just wasn't built for mediocre lovers

and their easy going attempts at making the dry ice in my chest melt

What should I do when love is now interchangeable fast food that keeps me dehydrated?

All I wish to do is pour myself into the desert to recreate plush mountains

Holding my breath, waiting for the moment to echo how much I love him until the sounds no longer resemble despair but shouts of freedom

What do you do when love is a secret that I cannot share

Music banned from the vicinity of my chest cavity because

no one can read the Braille sheet music I carry

What do you do

when the speakers of a heart, ready to love,

has no choice but to stay on Mute?

≠

There have been days where my sheets

knew my secrets howled into new moons,

Where a heart awaiting transformation reflects on the burning sun

And comfort resided within thread counts that don't quantify.

≠

Reparations

Pentupalogy

I apologize to my:

Heart

for allowing it to dream in a galaxy that carried too much gravity to fly.

Incarcerating it to disallow it flow abundantly in love.

Sorry for keeping you so cold and enslaved to

what's the point hopeless soliloquy's of disbelief: He couldn't possibly be loving me.

Sorry to my heart, for I never meant to self inflict bruises of uncharted hope.

Bleeding onto sleeves that were stain proof and leaving chunks of me to disintegrate into the floor.

Muffling cries of freedom each time my brain stood as your captor

I only meant to keep you safe,

Instead I left you exasperated for working so hard

Excitement no longer plays in the rhythm of skipped beats of amorous exhilaration

Instead somber symphonies of woe melodically mimic my reasoning

Be free to live fearlessly

I apologize to my **brain**

Working on over drive for survival

Canceling humanity for robotic responses and miscalculated mannerisms

Forcing words to remain unsaid

Overwriting emotional outbursts for calm collection

Confusing distrust

for the inability to believe that this love we once shared

was a possibility

I am sorry for programming emotions to never escape my souls windowsills

for vulnerability to be obtainable for me

it's a shameful disease

I prefer to keep in quarantine

Wondering do you really need the most broken and jagged parts of me?

Dear brain who syncs to my heart

in relentlessly wishing,

love to come my way

to finally be free in reciprocation

Unable to reset my mentality to open book loving,

misunderstanding the necessity to be read diligently

into the depth of my trust and abandonment issues

Preventing my lips, from requesting needs

due to consistent years of proof that

my needs have no validity

Dear brain we have pre-construed negative possibilities

living in invisibility

Let us be half full instead of fully empty, let us

live offensively instead of defensively

Open thyself in love and free creativity,

Be free to live fearlessly,

To my **belly**,

I have allowed others to mistreat you

until it affected me psychologically

Placing bounties on my beauty,

left me hunting for your elimination

Angry at the growing against my will,

no one speaks of the hormonal effect of birth control pills

Dear roundness

that filled men's hands like flower beds in the desert,

looked at like the cloud of the sky, fulfilling their parched lips

You have given me a pouch to hide my insecurities

and take blows of self disgust

I apologize to staring at you sideways in the mirror,

refusing to take accountability into action - men

have provided pleasure to my horrified belly button

To remind me no part of me isn't perfect, plushness

I prefer to feed you doses of admiration

than allow battered words to bruise my bravado.

I caress you in appreciation just as he has admired your softness,

Be free to live voluptuously,

I apologize to my **feet**,

That have bled silently, covering up the cuts

so no one can see through pedicured toes the roughness my heels,

Due to placing myself in all the wrong shoes

Unsure where to step next,

Confusing the right paths for harmful nail beds

Not once protecting the extra skin and removing it

to lead myself into dangerous locations of exposure to shards of confusion

Unaccountable to walking down my own valley,

placing other people's shadows

as my heels attempting to save them in exchange for many emotional deaths (disappointments)

Ignoring the cramps of carrying too much impersonal weight.

Be free to live vicariously through your own bare feet,

Lastly, I apologize to my **shoulders**...

For carrying the crosses of others who would consistently sacrifice me as their lamb,

I have ruined my spine with the anxiety I have self imposed,

Allowing no one to take off the loads,

I have been too preoccupied with placing capes of a hero

to remind myself of my own rights of humanity within,

Carrying numerous styled bags overloaded with unresolved issues

Hoarding clutches and body bags that created further humps at the rounding my shoulders

I am sorry for taking on more than nature intended to

believing the chips on my shoulders were to be the largest of boulders,

I have been a canyon

for denial and tundra for resolution,

the glaciers on my shoulders prevented me from floating.

Feel free to live lightly

As I release baggage in order to apologize to my body,

Living voluptuously fearless.

Accept my apology wholeheartedly.

He touches my belly as if he knew my insecurities lied there exposed for him to see all to himself. I've been told to lose weight my whole life and still here he is touching parts of me that were always picked apart. His hands made me feel like art. Beautiful.

A Whole Damn Year

It took- and takes-

Everything from within to keep the war path clear.

It's taken a whole damn year

To reconstruct the bricks that have been beaten into dust

with my eyes blinded and back turned

The foundation was brittle from the commencement and I never noticed

Sadly it still pains me

How easily thieves come take your most prized possessions

when the door is open for them to enter,

Barricades lowered and walls reconstructed to be open windows

Why creep in?

Awaiting lowered shields to bring in the wrecking ball.

I don't love him

nor need him anymore

that is the first pour of cement back into my lost sentiment of self

Comfort in the discomfort of solitude

Unable to rehash sense of self

when did my soul become ash ?

I await the cracks to fill and dry

the seasons come and

detract from efforts To solidify,

Pain is not unfamiliar

although this Temple on the outside resembles finished concrete

I - crumble and crunch under the weight

I carry each time I am left in the deep

A year to remodel my body, yet the insides have yet to recover

Self reparation is harder without a general contractor's expertise

So I bang, missing screws into sheet rock

plastering it just from the outside, the hollowness,

looks pretty but spring rain has revealed a few weak spots in my roof.

The summer heat is scorching,

melting the tar showing that there are shingles loose

Autumn hurricanes came and blew

everything to pieces

exposing the previous debauchery of fraudulent handymen

And he- comes to peruse a possible purchase

yet he hasn't seen the disclaimer- PROCEED WITH CAUTION

Haven't you noticed I am still under construction's unsettled dust? My frames rust ? Have you confused me for a new home when the mold although unseen - I could kill you- silently

It took a whole damn year just to repaint a presentable grimace on the outside yet it takes a team of solitude to restore the natural damages inside...

I have been repossessed involuntarily, foreclosed as I keep coming out undervalued

Attempting to reinvest in myself and coming up short. The last quinary

I rebuild walls and re-frame doors adding additional locks yet attempting to paint colors of cheeriness inside when gloom remains within trap doors leading to the posterior

I contain myself in the pool of bravery attempting to not drown in my misery of needing companionship yet the tiles seem to come loose when prospects peruse.

Looking great on the surface, Yet rehashing tools,

Taking years to repair my body

I met a coward today,

as she looked back at me on the frozen lake.

The blueish hue of my skin, made who I used to be,

Unrecognizable.

Pain has made me self-engulf hope

translating it to a result that has yet to happen,

Fighting to stay afloat

when I cannot chemically arrange the carbon dioxide of toxic experiences

Into oxygen filled hope,

factually it has been a repeated failure in different attempts,

I chose chemistry each time,

when in reality, life,

dear coward,

is quantum physics,

not exactly a sure result,

only factors and potential outcomes.

Love will always be my reason to Live, although it has caused me many deaths, dear frozen gladiator, its time to arm yourself, to unbear arms.

ICE BOX

Dear estranged lover,

I am not placed on

MY self built table

for you

to pick apart

your favorite pieces of me,

my culture is

not for you

to dissect and savor individually,

foolishly surveying which is your favorite flag

or which tongue you wish me to whisper, this melange is not made for your catering. I am no morsel,

to be fed to an eager set of ignorant lips.

I am the combination

of an inedible

whole meal to be lodged

down your awestruck

t h r o a t.

Hope less

There was something about watching him as he slept - a mesmerizing peace

that would not let me waste time sleeping beside him.

Caressing his head and rubbing his ears to prevent him from returning to the reality that all things come to an end and even if it isn't today - it would come

Something about watching him without his facade on display

and his burdens left outside the house that made me skip a beat

as he snored in restful slumber - not once taking my eyes off of him

contemplating a paragon in the darkness

And he said

we will never be nothing,

that was loves temporary lie as it dropped down his lips,

I, eating the leftovers of hope,

as it slowly digested to reality,

nutrients of truth now empty...**you left me starving**

The End is the Beginning

Reaching the seasons coldest sunset,

where the eclipse is all that can be seen from love given,

lost and never received

Gazing at the frozen pools of romantic notions that no longer dispense from a beating ticker,

I love you's

are slipped into my ears

but never reach a temperature to revival,

Eyelashes do not bat

Although, for an instance I falter,

I wanted to be the reason the world looked green in your eyes,

instead of the frozen desert I remain in,

I wanted to

tilt your orbit away from the black hole

we choose

to oppositely reside in,

as if the reflective energy of our eyes

were sufficient to change how we see earth,

Yet signs of compatibility with inaction come up short,

I wanted to be human again,

Longingly wishing

the clock would slow down and

the boulders on our shoulders would be minced into a new belief,

My heart attempted to defrost at your sight and still,

the footsteps echoed

through the empty palace,

not good enough, to be chosen first by you,

Failing to continue a trek of life without you, each time I catch my breath,

you remind me why my knees have their indentations,

Begging for love has been our custom

not once being granted our wish to be free,

displayed and told of fables of my truth, unmoved,

sailing away, my soul left, on the glacier to watch your disappearance,

I only wanted eternity instead I received death...

-I wanted to love you-

I still have days that I miss you,

as soon as your warmth leaves my fingertips, backs are turned, words remain unsaid and time resumes its count.

I, now a distant memory framed within text messages.

Watching you walk away, as if love in unmet eyes haven't confessed,

attempting to place myself back into civilization from this Love Purgatory.

I don't want to be free.

Resentfully living in a world of expectations
that lack of hope crowds an inspired heart

covered in the what fors?

Glass half empty aspirations,

Silence has left me

bleeding   ice   cubes

anger and sadness

to be served in cocktails of foolishness.

Pitter patter

I desire him

To the point my nails dig in to

His back

I moan and wrap my legs around him

He grunts in my ear

And I remind myself

we are the drying tears

Of yesterday

Platonic now

Strange to not say

I love you and

Mean it

Forever in a way we

Never figured out to be

On nights like this,

the moon is the brightest light in the sky,

the city but a sketch of civilization,

the stars as brightly embossed in the night.

> The cold is comforting, granting me peace that no one has been able to provide, no hands to console solitude, no lies to draw snowflake hearts illusions around my crown, for once, freedom was bone chillingly homey.

Snowmen deformed in the blizzard of emotional unavailability where I reside.

For once, silence was a dream I could materialize as the pain no longer howled in the wind.

I was truly, reborn from the outside in.

Realizations of an ice queen at 5:06 am when no one else is around but myself, God, and the universe.

IF I TOLD HIM,

EVERY TIME I HEARD A SONG WE HAVE MADE LOVE TO,

on that day, where the world melted away,

and sex had a change of heart and love somehow found it's way in this shallow lie.

Where my eyes, became the Rivers I always wanted to follow so I could dive into his ocean,

Would he

comprehend

that one sided love on opposing circumferences

does me more harm than good,

What a life, to believe heartbreak is the fairy tale ending specifically designed,

What a lie,

that happiness came in his custom imprinted name.

Etched into a heart filled with unsolicited feelings,

Would he even comprehend my intelligible sentences?

I speak in verb form traced on the pages of visual proof.

The fact that I keep asking questions to everyone except you, shows how embarrassing it is for me to express my emotion.

The frozen matter solidified around my lungs has left me motionless verbally,

I am not sorry that you too, see how our past lives have been interconnected and oddly enough, I would wait a thousand life times for you.

Dear Love, I have the audacity to believe that I deserve my own endings, filled with fairy beginnings, a once upon a time that had no *The End* to give birth to

broken mirrors and betrayal

But how many women can hear your silence

and interpret the view reflected in the window of your soul?

My eyes still dance in the moonlight

away from the gaze you hold

as you capture the crumbs of love

I disheveled into your palms

Wanting for permanence of love

to remain photographed

for replays into the unwritten future

Where I love you as I love me

and we can love us until loving

becomes a sense of self within the other

And half loves

fall into the dusk of insufficient reality

to be a lie never told as we lie within the other

Crave me fully

So I can satiate you with droplets of me

onto your syllables and each time you draw breath

I am the soliloquy of your conscious unveiled

Dear love

I have reached out fingers

to grasps the stars and cradle

the pre-construed constellation seemingly so close

Surprisingly so distant

Unable to cradle the babe of hope that is locked

in the darkest dungeons

of forgotten frolicker-y

that is my heart fighting the layers of self-preservation,

loud enough for my ears to ring with the voice,

free me

I did not have familiarity with this woman

Ego elephant

Pacing vehemently in my brain waves

As pride and vulnerability fight for first place

I loved you so long by myself

imagine if I saved it all for me?

As a poet

to be an afterthought of love to others

is like not having a writing instrument

to etch inspiration into permanent oblivion

To be the last option

in a loved one's mind

is to run out of words to describe happiness

or deep sadness when overflowed

Unspoken Soliloquies meant for conversation

Random Love gazing

I have been gazing into the stars,

shuttled in the pupils of your soul

Wondering

does love come in your size?

Does it grow in the way you walk

Because my heart,

has been sending an SOS to you

every time you reach close proximity

have you heard my Morse code plea?

When eyes meet and record each second

Of the comforting frequency you transfer to me

Unable to write enough words

to define how your aura creates campfires within

I've been cold through the winters of disapproval of love,

being what anyone could offer to me

Yet, only you give me this craving of empirical reparation

I've been confusing my heartbreak to be interchangeable with sexual saving

And still amid days where I cannot see through dark clouds,

you emit the brightest of rays

maybe I confuse this display as nature taking its course

But physical conversations are enough

to revisit the magnitude of how much you mean to me

My love language may not be loud enough for you

to comprehend how deep in my veins you run in me

Doesn't love come in your size

so i can wear it over my chest,

to feel the embrace I keep tightly laced in my memories

Of how without sex you reached an unfamiliar depth to me

Sleep misses your body heat engrossing me

I have loved you for centuries and still without any logic

I continue to doubt the essence that fills butterflies in my stomach

every time my recognition is filled with our remembrance

Sadly I still wonder in the form of actions,

do you really love me the way I love you ?

Would you be ready to mutate with gills to know how deep this ocean of love is?

Can I

re-buffer your soul to reflect your raw inner Beauty,

am I so helplessly a fool for what could be ?

I leave galaxies in the time spent between us

and the unsaid stars remaining undiscovered...

I miss you

even if we have yet to separate into the light years of tomorrow

Questions

I never ask in this mission of discovery...a lover's soliloquy

DEAR SNOWMEN

The moment you decided my love was not enough for you,

Did you feel free? Did it bring you light and joyfulness?

Did she smile at you the same way I never could?

Was I easy to forget in your changing of seasons?

- I never told you did I -

That these blizzards had every single memory of us imprinted in the walls of contempt that I carried.

Sobs weren't loud enough nor frequent enough to heal the sorrow.

My seasons never changed from winter.

I was cold, from the hunger in my ribs as I contemplated my self-worth,

Fickle promises of forever dripping from the ashes of my fingertips.

I love in eternities as you, recorded these moments, so as to not forget or to easily delete them altogether?

I used to ask myself while looking at the snow angels that disperse in the moonlight, was it all I lie?

I was guilty, of staying too long, expecting Godliness and not knowing when to let the rainy days go.

But how, can I not attempt to place rainbows at their feet, when it felt like home.

Dear Snowmen,

I loved each one of you, at the moment you were the one and may still be,

But an aching heart bedazzled in carbon dioxide does not know the difference.

Sometimes, I bitterly catch snowflakes of regret, wishing you had told me earlier, so hope would not have been a conspiracy I would have prescribed to.

Undeserving to my greatness you all agreed in unison, at times aloud.

Slowly placing the shards into a crown, I realized:

I was too intense, too much, draped in royal affliction

For you.

≠

That is the one thing I missed the most was spending hours on the phone saying nothing but taking in, each others living spaces,

using time as currency towards adding love

into an adventure to heal loneliness

Your voice

the very stimuli I never knew I needed

for this growing addiction

Melting the mosaic of frozen icicles built on the walls of a fragile heart

You are what soul mates are made of

In movies where she finally gets Prince Charming

≠

Since when, did Love become a prison you don't want life sentences to?

We will always be friends - but will we ever be public lovers?

You have filled a place so vastly in my heart that

I am unable to let someone else move in

your idiosyncrasies are still here,

hoarding un-relivable memories

how can I discard each piece of you that I gave, from me

When friendship becomes a stigma,

I start to despise the silence in which my tears are invisible

the pain in my heart isn't loud enough,

for you to recognize my love isn't small enough to fit in that box

where only bits of you and I - click together in misshapen puzzle pieces –

this is not where peace is left appeasing this bitter truth

Embarrassed at how much love I've poured into a well

Lost in your alphabet soup of friends who are devoured and forgotten letters –

I don't wish to float on the surface of you

so I sink in the loneliness of loving you

Your love consumes me like quicksand

that dives into tundras, the happiest lie I have ever told myself, in a paused happy ever after

that never started with a proper story

a tale untold

I have been drunk in the stupor of lustful libations - drink every remnant drop,

down dehydrated lips - redefining - thirst -you put me on

now I can't get off

Pretending that I cannot take you whole

when I have taken you in whole

didn't I beg for more of you to be left here comfortably to Rest In Peace

I have been accustomed to marathon runners

practicing their ideas while running circles of pre-love

against my heart until they win their way out

leaving caution behind

complacent to customers and not clients

signing long term contracts to end less beginnings

Love Rears its ugly head

I have always feared how I love you

Silently soaking the rays of you until the ozone layer of my pastry heart flaked in its own crust -

allowing vulnerability to be left agape for you

to enjoy the sweetest part of me

Un   offered

yet served up

until you tire of me

still I attempt to keep all the leftovers together

Have you seen me as a chapel

looking through stained glass windows,

I call you a prophetic prototype

to what love is meant to look like

Touch-ably Immortal

I have had prayers answered

that carry your name

A demon to provide exorcisms

requested to purge my need

to possess you fully

Rename you as an object of my belonging

You don't know the fires

I have baptized myself in

to create a curse to your name and run from the butterflies

that have become bats of doubt

in my evenings

You atone me

in the lashes of karma

within my deadly sins that all revolve around loving you

Wading in stagnant waters to be named Mine as Yours and reborn into US

Unable to cloth sheep into a wolf they could never be, preying on paupers until deemed throneless princes

I could never be a queen to ^{un}rightful heirs

Saying I love you,

falls short to the times

I can write you into

future and fiction simultaneously,

So my lips preserve energy

to create an infinite time machine

where love resides,

in every century

Learning to bathe

in the rays of darkness

covered by moonlight

Sight becomes inverted in the daytime

clarity is blurred

through the snow storms

You will always be

my favorite hallway

where trespassing into each other emotions

was an addiction

still denied entry

I watch from the Windows

remembering the memories

left inside the dust particles

created by the sun

I want this love to free me

while saving us

mutually into a new-found existence

Remembering past lives

yet creating new memories

I tire

of swallowing emotions

suppressed into nothingness

I tire of pouring myself into hollow wells,
I require a love that flows into an aquifer
until both of us overflow onto a new source of expansive fluidity.

Under this undefinable heart of glacier

Is a warmth that has lit men into incense, displaying the remnants of what was in forgotten dreams. I've incinerated my men into lustful ashes of what never will be

Deeper lies a fire

confused to be smoke,

where Love encendió resides

awaiting he who can take the flames and get purified instead of burned.

He who can take this hurricane and find a home in my tumultuous sea.

Under these glaciers

is a burning Atlantis waiting to be free

People ask if I met someone in Zanzibar for me to love it so

-I did- my true self without the pain of yesterday.

Colorin Colorado Este Cuento Se Ha Acabado

Thank you

I have felt like a flailing leaf in the winters of yesterday, supported by the branches of love: friendships, family and sisterhood in surprising ways.

I have accustomed myself to solace, silenced pain, self engulfed hurt, and forceful healing.

So thank you, to those I shunned during my hurt who refused to leave, those who were present when I needed them most, those who validated my feelings when I couldn't do so myself.

I would not be here today, after these 5 years of growth and healing.

To those who loved me back into healing with kindness, patience, and resistance, I thank you.

A special thank you to: my mother who keeps helping me rebuild my foundation.

My grandmother who lets me hit the wall and says there is another sunny path waiting for you.

My artistic friends who have blessed me with their skills and time in making my covers: Justin and Sarah.

To all of those who have been in this journey.

Dear reader, I humbly extend my gratitude for your time, investment, and curiosity into the Soliloquy of an Ice Queen. May their be hope, even if it is a sliver of light, in the darkness of days and extension of the simple joys you already contain.

Thank you

TO THE WOMAN WHO FORGOT SHE IS A GOD_{DESS}

Perfect in the Image of the universe's creation

How could you forget yourself, in the shadows of mortal men,

That YOU are the Creator of their existence ?

Placing their brittle egos on celestial pedestals,

only

YOU are worthy of ?

Dear diosa que se olvida the very essence she is made of - don't you ever wonder why the womxn is the most attacked and disrespected being ?

To recognize your magic is to fight history, to self love is a blasphemy to those of menial stature

Bonje beni existans nou as we do the miracles only we are capable of.

Loving others as our entity would

Dear God$_{dess}$ who has forgotten why we were hung as witches

Can anyone else majestically

Carry burdens and sacrifice for love as we are wired to?

Can anyone else brew potions of healing in midnight strolls

and raise households of once broken people ?

Who else

can revive and bring life

- to shattered hearts and broken winged lovers -

can you not see yourself as the light that burns through the darkness?

HOPE

is made in the outlines of our decisions to be as we are

- a movement -

rebellion of cookie cutter ideologies changes civilization

To the woman

who hasn't taken time to flirt back

with her Goddess like imper-flection

May society not limit how important your existence is,

may the silence of your suffering never be comfortable,

and may

You love yourself

wholehearted as the universe Intended you to be- perfect in its image

> Pa bliye ou se majik
>
> No te olvides que eres magica
>
> Do not forgot that you - are magic

Epilogue

Legacy, I want to relive the feeling of solidarity in growth, hope, love, and heartbreak.

Knowing that it never buried me in a coffin of snow storms.

But that I become the hail beating against the windows of denial, self-doubt, and fear of never being enough,

I want to know and remind anyone in their triumph and losses.

That just like I am enough.

So are you,

Always.

Notes from the Author
What is Krik Krak?

Krik Krak is a Haitian Creole saying introducing a story before it is told.

The story teller says **Krik**, and the listener say **Krak** and then the telling begins.

This is how my father and I used to go about during our car rides as I was a child.

Passing down fables and stories, he was my audible before it existed.

Colorin Colorado Este Cuento Se Ha Acabado?

I know this as a Puerto Rican phrase for when a story has ended.

The story teller usually says this to signify the ending.

If interested in working with me, following my journey, and/or seeing additional work:

Instagram : @lyszflo

Facebook: https://www.facebook.com/lyszobservatory/

Twitter: https://twitter.com/lyszflo

Goodreads: https://www.goodreads.com/author/show/18981478.Lysz_Flo

Email : lyszflo@gmail.com

Website: https://www.lyszflo.com

www.ingramcontent.com/pod-product-compliance
Lightning Source LLC
Chambersburg PA
CBHW071345080526
44587CB00017B/2978